The Saving of St Davids Cathedral

The story of the decline of
Wales' principal cathedral
after the Reformation
and its restoration
between 1790 and 1901

The Saving of St Davids Cathedral

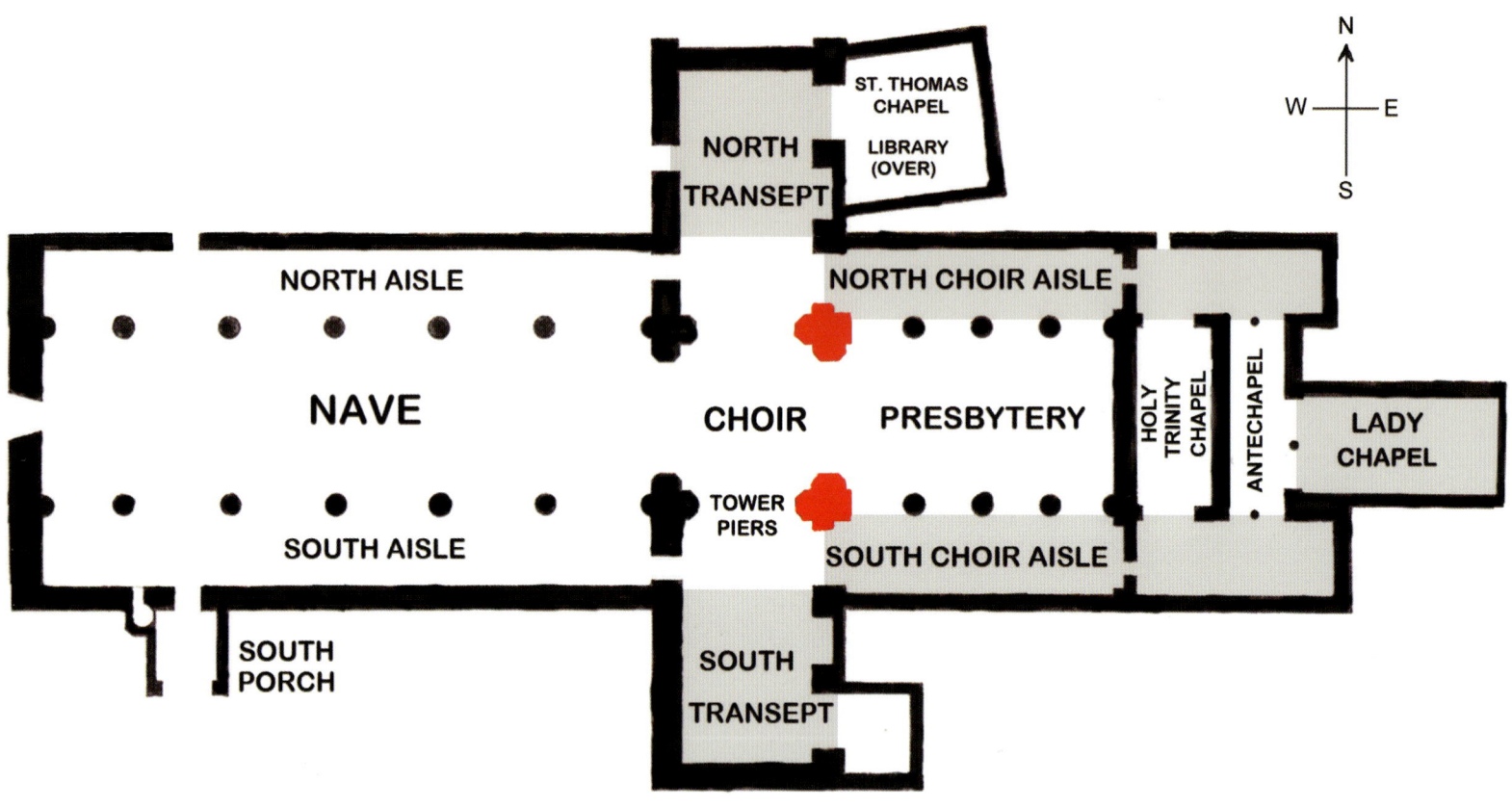

1 Ground plan of the cathedral. The two tower piers which collapsed in 1220 are shown in red. The grey shading denotes the roof areas which were stripped of their lead in 1648 or earlier.

INTRODUCTION

'While the entire building was reported to be in a state of the most severe dilapidation, and some portions actually in ruins, the greatest immediate danger was to be apprehended from the Tower, the crushed condition of two of whose sustaining piers rendered its fall an event by no means improbable – a catastrophe which would probably involve the destruction of a large portion of the Church.'

From Second Report on the State of the Fabric of St David's Cathedral by Geo. Gilbert Scott 1869

There have been times in the past when St Davids Cathedral was not the magnificent building we see today, but was for some two hundred years in a semi- ruinous condition and even a potential danger to those who worshipped there. It is difficult for present day visitors to appreciate this. They assume, reasonably enough, the cathedral has always looked much as it does at the moment. Nothing could be further from the truth. A glance at the illustration on the back cover shows how the West Front looked at the end of the eighteenth century – propped up with massive wooden shores. The chequered history of the building is only briefly mentioned in modern guide books and none enters into any great detail.

The valley site on which the cathedral is built had two disadvantages: it was both sloping and boggy. On one side is the river Alun and on the other is the steeply-sloping land leading up to the city. The original builders must have decided to follow the slope of the valley bottom as can be seen on the floor of the nave. There was little they could do about the drainage of the site. Since architectural knowledge was still fairly experimental then, the foundations put in were never adequate to give the structure the necessary stability. The consequence of this was that the tower and the west front gave continual problems for hundreds of years until the nineteenth century. One of the priorities for the Victorian restorers was to install a proper drainage system.

The purpose of this account is to explore the many vicissitudes which the cathedral has suffered since its foundation in the twelfth century. What were the problems and how were they surmounted? Who were the people involved and how was the money raised? The surviving documents in the form of letters, newspaper articles, drawings and photographs throw a fascinating light on the clergy, architects and builders concerned. A ground plan of the cathedral is shown in *Fig. 1* so that the reader can follow the various areas mentioned in the text.

In considering the gradual decline and subsequent restoration of the cathedral fabric, there has always been one overriding factor to take into account: its remote position at the extreme, in the minds of some people, western tip of South Wales, which indeed has led to doubts about its very existence (see page 18). Access by road would have been difficult until modern times, but there was the nearby harbour of Porth Clais to bring in heavy and bulky material on coasters. Even as late as 1901, a cathedral guide book was advising visitors to take the train to Haverfordwest (16 miles distant)), spend the night there, and travel on to St Davids the next day.

2 Interior of the tower showing, on the left, the original west arch (rounded) and, on the right, one of the three replacement arches (pointed) built after the collapse in 1220. Two of the sets of black tie rods inserted to stabilize the tower in Victorian times can also be seen (author photo)

Earlier Period

The Cathedral we see today was begun under Bishop Peter de Leia in the year 1181. From the very start it suffered two serious reversals. In 1220, the Tower collapsed because its two eastern supports (piers) gave way due to inadequate foundations. In this St Davids was not unique: there were other collapses at Winchester Cathedral (1120), Lincoln (1237) and even as late as 1861 at Chichester. The original Tower was only one third of the height of the present one, but nevertheless the devastation must have been considerable. The rebuilding should have started from new foundations with four new piers. Instead, the quicker and cheaper solution was adopted of retaining the surviving western piers and only rebuilding the fallen ones. The result can still be seen today.

The arch between the western piers facing the nave is rounded in the Norman style whereas the other three arches have the pointed form of the Gothic *(Fig. 2)*. Moreover, the long-term consequence of this short cut was more than just stylistic. It left serious structural weaknesses in the Tower which threatened the whole building. Despite these problems, two extra stages were later added to the height of the Tower, so increasing the risks, which were further compounded by the hanging of heavy bells. In their authoritative history of the Cathedral published in 1856, Jones and Freeman[1] do not shrink from castigating those in charge of the rebuilding after 1220:

'Certainly no architects ever displayed a smaller degree of wisdom than those who were about to reconstruct it. For instead of rebuilding the whole lantern [i.e. the tower] from the foundation, the old western arch, though itself far from secure, was retained……The result of this is that the tower has been in a condition which may be called dangerous for six hundred years, and it is wonderful that none of the successive additions to its height have fairly brought it down once more.'

If the worst had happened, the Tower would probably have collapsed in a westerly direction on the nave and the results do not bear contemplation. The Cathedral would have been reduced to a picturesque ruin like Tintern Abbey. Mercifully, there were no disasters until a long-term solution was devised in the nineteenth century.

Only twenty four years after the collapse of the Tower, the area had the misfortune to be struck by an earthquake in 1248, causing further damage. The details of this are not clear but it is more than likely that the outward leaning of the nave pillars seen today is a consequence [2]. But another contributing factor was probably the steep pitch of the roof at the time (still to be seen on the west face of the tower), which would have exerted outward pressure on the nave walls. To counteract the instability, the massive and rather ugly buttresses on the north side of the nave were built, but not until the middle of the sixteenth century. These have now been ingeniously incorporated into the new cloister.

Later the various eastern chapels were completed, so that by the time of the Reformation (1530s), the Cathedral would have looked externally much as it does today. Exceptions would have been the West Front which was in its original form *see Fig.8* and the East Window of the Presbytery which replaced the original lancets. The first Protestant bishop in the new Church of England (which included Wales) was William Barlow (1536-48). It was he who moved the bishop's residence from the Palace at St Davids to Abergwilli, Carmarthenshire and he also wished to recreate the Cathedral there. The Chapter disagreed and they prevailed. It was at this time, despite all the turmoil in the religious life of the country, that the magnificent oak ceiling in the nave was built[3] (*Fig. 3*). At the same time, though because of the Reformation, the Cathedral lost one of its main sources of income: pilgrims' offerings at St David's shrine.

3 Carved oak ceiling in the nave from the first half of the sixteenth century (author photo)

The Saving of St Davids Cathedral

The Period of Decay

The Civil War saw the next major event in the Cathedral's history that began a process of decline in its condition which was only effectively stopped two hundred years later. Pembrokeshire was largely Royalist at the outset of the war, but after many battles in the county, the Parliamentarians finally gained control after the siege of Pembroke Castle in the summer of 1648[4]. There is a record which shows that in August a troop of dragoons was sent to the cathedral to remove 3000 '*weight*' of lead from the roofs[5]. If 'weight' means pounds weight, that amounts to 1.3 tons and is only a small fraction of the total weight of lead (of the order of 100 tons). It is also far less than would have covered the exposed areas which were apparently the Lady Chapel, both Choir Aisles and both

4 Simulation on a SE view of the lead roofing and windows missing after the Civil War (author photo)

5 Left: North Choir Aisle in the 1850's, roofless and with arches into the Presbytery blocked up (Jones and Freeman P.142). Right: as it appears now (author photo).

Transepts. It is unclear how and when the much larger amount of lead was actually removed, but there is a suggestion that it was taken much earlier at the time of the Reformation[6]. As well as stripping the roofs, the soldiers smashed windows, damaged the organ and allegedly removed the largest bell from the Tower by taking it out through the wall[7]! The full extent of the devastation has been simulated in *Fig. 4*. Instead of replacing the missing roofs, the Cathedral authorities decided to keep out the weather by blocking up the arches of the Presbytery and abandoning the more eastern chapels and aisles. The effect is shown in *Fig 5*. The southern Tower arch was also filled with masonry, partly to support the unsafe Tower. The western arch had been filled for the same purpose one hundred years earlier[8]. The effect of all this work must have made the areas of the Choir and Presbytery dark and claustrophobic, a situation which was not rectified until the Victorian restoration of George Gilbert Scott, two hundred years later.

In January, 1660 a petition[9] was sent to the new 'King', Charles II, asking that those who had been responsible for removing the lead 'be obliged to make such recompense as shall be thought fit'. There does not seem to have been any response from Whitehall. In any case the date must be in question because Charles II was only proclaimed King in May, 1660.

The Chapter did arrange to have the Transepts releaded in 1696[10] after an interval of forty eight years, still leaving the other areas open to the elements. Expenditure on the Fabric during much of the eighteenth century seems to have been confined to minor maintenance. The wooden roofs in the Choir Aisles of course began to rot and eventually collapsed. The engraving reproduced in *Fig. 6* shows all too well the state of the building. The stone vaults of Holy Trinity Chapel and the Antechapel did survive, but the vault of the Lady Chapel was not so fortunate and added to the ruination by falling in 1775[11].

6 View from the NE in the late eighteenth century showing the ruinous state of the Lady Chapel (left) and the North Choir Aisle (centre). (Cathedral Library)

The Saving of St Davids Cathedral

Apparently, the Precentor (as the Dean was known until 1840) wished to take down an attractive boss in the vault which led to the collapse[12] *(Fig 7)*. The middle of the eighteenth century was, without doubt, the low point of the Cathedral's life as a building.

St Davids was not alone in becoming ill-maintained around this time. A W N Pugin[13] describes the neglect of Ely Cathedral: 'the water pouring through unclosed apertures in the covering , conveying water into the heart of the fabric' and 'the opening of fissures in the great western tower which…..are rapidly extending'. He goes on to say that the same observations apply to other great churches, including, Westminster Abbey.

7 View of the Lady Chapel after the collapse of its vault in 1775 (Cathedral Library)

Eighteenth Century Revival

There must have been continuing anxiety about the actual stability of the Cathedral towards the end of the eighteenth century, in particular the alarming outward lean of the West Front. In 1779 John Calvert from Swansea was commissioned to make a survey. His rather vague and short report[14] suggests buttressing to support the West Front at a cost of only £110 and trussing to strengthen the Tower floor for £70. It appears that the buttressing of the West Front may have been accomplished, as we shall see shortly (page 9). At this time it was apparently the custom for one member of the Chapter to be responsible for the maintenance of the building, the Master of the Fabric. The position was only held for one year and there were only occasional reappointments. The records show that the first decision at each annual Chapter meeting was to appoint a new Master of the Fabric and that in the last twenty years of the eighteenth century there were sixteen Masters. This arrangement seems unlikely to have been conducive to providing the vigorous action which was sorely needed, but matters were about to take a turn for the better. In 1788, Samuel Horsley was appointed Bishop. That he was a man of firm convictions can be gauged from this quotation from a speech on slavery he made to the House of Lords in 1806:

> 'What can the utmost humanity of the master do for the slave? He may feed him well, clothe him well, work him moderately; but, my lords, nothing that the master can do for his slave, short of manumission, can reinstate him in the condition of man. But the Negro Slave in the West Indies!—my lords, you may pamper him every day with the choicest viands—you may lay him to repose at night on beds of roses—but, with all this, he is not in the condition of man; he is nothing better than a well-kept horse. This is my notion of slavery.'

He was also a man of considerable academic attainments, as a mathematician and a theologian. He was a Fellow, later Secretary, of the Royal Society and had engaged in fierce controversy with Joseph Priestley about the doctrine of the Trinity. Horsley lost no time in writing a stern letter[15] to the Chapter in July, 1789:

> 'Upon a visit of curiosity to St Davids last summer, I was more struck than I can easily express with the ruined appearance of the Cathedral, which is too evidently in a state to demand the serious and immediate attention of those to whom the care and custody of this edifice properly belongs…….The assistance of the public must be asked and there is little room to doubt but it will be obtained……It will previously be necessary that the extent of the work to be done and the amount of expense should be ascertained. For this purpose I most earnestly recommend to the present Chapter not to separate without passing an Order for an immediate survey of the building and an estimate of the expense of the repair……..I purpose to visit my Cathedral the ensuing summer when I doubt not of your cheerful concurrence in the measures that may be necessary.'

The Saving of St Davids Cathedral

8 The west front of the cathedral as depicted by Pugin showing the temporary shoring (courtesy Roy Lewis)

9 Drawing of the western end of the Nave by Pugin showing Nash's plan for shoring the leaning West Front with timber cased in stone buttresses. Note the leaning and cracked nave pillars and also the tapered facing on the lower part of the front (courtesy Roy Lewis)

With hindsight, this letter can be seen as a pivotal point in the history of the Fabric, when the inexorable decline was reversed and gave way to gradual restitution during the next 100 years.

The Chapter hastened to ask John Nash, who later become the famous Regency architect, to make a survey. A subscription list was opened and one entry for five guineas was from Nash himself although there are doubts about whether he actually paid[16]! An initial total of £1289 was raised and the final amount came to £1931. At this time Nash was practising in Carmarthen, after an inauspicious start to his career in London involving bankruptcy and divorce, before he returned to England in 1796 to become the famous Regency architect. He had built up a reputation over eleven years for his designs of villas, bridges, churches and public buildings in South Wales. At the time he was forty years old and determined to make a name for himself. Nash persuaded the Chapter to commission a series of fourteen large drawings depicting the Cathedral before and after restoration. He engaged the services of Auguste-Charles Pugin (father of the architect and designer A.W.N. Pugin) to make these at a cost of fifteen guineas each. The drawing reproduced in *Fig. 8* shows the original medieval West Front with the temporary shoring to support it before it was rebuilt to Nash's new design. It is unclear whether this shoring was put up as a result of the Calvert survey or whether it was emergency shoring put up by Nash before his own more permanent solution. The Front apparently had a lean from the vertical which has been stated as either twelve inches or two feet eleven inches. The second figure sounds scarcely credible.[16] The fundamental problem at the West Front was that the Norman foundations were quite inadequate, on the marshy ground, to support the Front or to resist the westward pressure of the nave arcade caused by the unstable Tower.

The survey[17] recommended rebuilding the upper part of the West Front and supporting it with two massive wooden shores encased in stone buttresses. There were to be new foundations going down ten feet including piles of 'Norway fir'. The Pugin drawing in *Fig 9* shows the proposals and also the shattering of the nave pillars. The lower part of the Front up to the main window was to have a tapered facing, ten inches thick at ground level and six inches at window level. The fenestration was to be completely changed with a single large window in perpendicular style replacing the multiple original windows.

10 Victorian photograph of Nash's West Front before it was replaced by Scott. Note the broken window and also the cantilevered plank for masons near the top of the Tower which to us looks very unsafe (see also Fig. 22) (Cathedral Library)

In addition, the sides of the gable end were to be topped by castellated turrets. The somewhat eclectic design is shown in *Fig.10* which is a photograph taken in Victorian times. In 1856, the scheme was bluntly described by the Cathedral historians Jones and Freeman[18] as 'the greatest blot in the whole building'!

It is unclear whether Nash was asked to deal solely with the West Front. The reason for this is that his specifications for the West Front are headed 'No. 5'. What were the other four (or more) specifications? They have not survived, but they very likely dealt with all the other parts of the Cathedral because one of the Pugin drawings *(Fig. 11)* shows a complete south elevation with major changes in addition to those for the West Front. He seemed to be proposing a new large window in the South Transept, rebuilding the ruined eastern end with a new roof lines and the Tower crack repaired. Quite clearly the Chapter must have decided such a major work was beyond their means, but there is evidence that one other building in the Cathedral grounds was modified by Nash.

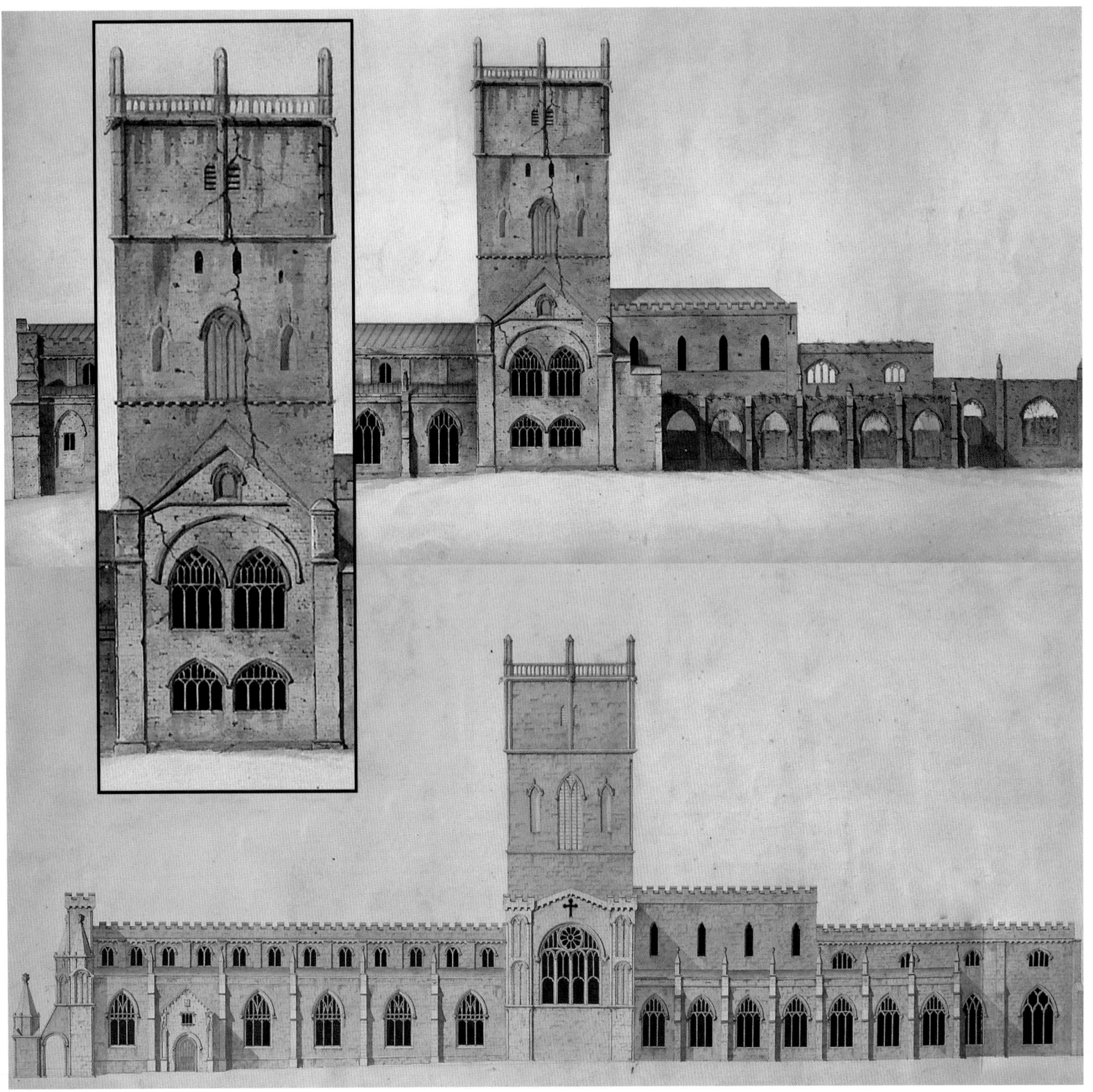

11 Two south elevations drawn by Pugin for Nash. Above before any changes, with the ominous crack in the tower and the windowless east end. Below seems to show proposals for a transformation of the whole building including the west end (which was accomplished), a new window in the south transept, and remodelled east end (which were not done) (courtesy Roy Lewis)

12 Water colour by Pugin of the precinct from the SW as it was in the 1790's after Nash's work was finished. It shows the rebuilt West Front and also the new Chapter House with its incongruous tower blocking the view of the nave (courtesy Roy Lewis)

One of the Pugin drawings *(Fig 12)* shows the rather incongruous rectangular building in the southwest corner of the grounds, which had originally been a workshop for those working on repairing the Cathedral and later served as the Cathedral School. Nash was asked to convert this into a Chapter House[16] and *Fig 12* also depicts the chimney disguised as a tower which he devised. As a Chapter House, it had only a short life and was demolished in 1829. Although Nash had dealt with the pressing problem of preventing the collapse of the West Front, there still remained the dangerous Tower and the dilapidated Eastern Chapels.

Nash points out in his report on the West Front[17], that the nearby harbour at Porth Clais *(Fig.13)* is the best route for bringing in bulky materials and rather touchingly tries to help the impoverished locals by recommending that:

> 'It will be expected that the contractor shall send the Portland stone and other materials in their rude state in order that the inhabitants of the City of St Davids may be benefitted as much as possible by the money to be expended in these erections.'

13 Porth Clais harbour in the nineteenth century with three coasters at the quay. Note the damaged breakwater (courtesy Carole Lloyd)

To make his survey and supervise the work, Nash made a surprising number of visits to St Davids. He invoices for seventeen by himself (at 4 guineas) and four by his clerk (at 2 guineas). The contract was awarded in April 1791 to James Yates from Bromyard, Herefordshire as stone mason and Joseph Mathias from Haverfordwest as carpenter. Their respective estimates were £799 and £750[19]. Both agreed to bonds of £1500 each to finish the work by July, 1792, which seems a surprisingly short time. In the event, all did not go smoothly. Nash wrote[20] to the Chapter in 1793 complaining about Yates that:

> 'In spite of frequent threats and recommendations he has continued to execute his work in an unworkmanlike manner and depart from his contract. Stone of all sorts without attending to soundness or colour has been used. Cramps have been omitted, workmanship of the most inferior sort, the design unattended to and a great deal of free stonework omitted.'

It is unclear whether Yates had to make good his misdemeanours, but there is a letter[21] written to the Chapter in 1816 noting the 'mouldering away' of the stone. Thomas Jones of Haverfordwest offers an acid treatment which will 'make it as durable as any stone'. The 'mouldering' was probably just the normal weathering of the local Old Red Sandstone from the quarry at Caerbwdy nearby *(Figs. 14, 20)* Nash's rebuilt West Front was to remain for just eighty years until the Victorians decided that there should be a third rebuilding, the version that we see today.

14 Sketch map showing the proximity of the two cliff-face quarries (Caerfai and Caerbwdy) and Porth Clais harbour

The financing of this major work appears to have been relatively smooth. We have already seen that £1931 had been raised from public subscription. The two contractors estimates came to £1549 while the actual expenditure was £2015[22]. However Nash's own fee caused considerable difficulty which was never properly resolved even well into the next century. According to I. Wyn Jones[16], the fee was £412, but he was paid just £150 in 1794. He agreed to a 'penal bond' for £500 (a form of IOU) which would pay him at a rate of 4% per annum. Nash seems to have been paid interest until 1797 when the Chapter accounts show no more payments. By this time he had established himself as a highly successful public figure. In 1816 the Chapter suddenly received a letter from a London solicitor asking for full payment[23]. This unexpected demand was greeted with consternation. Some canons thought the debt had been discharged while others were for a settlement. Only one was still alive who had been party to the original arrangement. In the event, Nash never brought a lawsuit against the Chapter nor did he receive any payment.

Just after the West Front was finished by Nash, the last invasion of Britain took place when the French landed near Fishguard in 1797. As in the Civil War, the Cathedral roofs were again regarded as a useful source of lead, but this time to be cast into bullets. While this story has been widely believed, there is only anecdotal evidence to support it and we may never know the truth. Nevertheless, a bag of lead bullets was said to have been found in a nearby farmhouse with a label stating they had been cast in 1797 for use against the French[24].

A few years later a survey was made of the Eastern chapels. Daniel Evans[25] noted in 1817 that the walls of Holy Trinity Chapel and the Antechapel were much decayed owing to the absence of roofs over the aisles. Canon Payne, Master of the Fabric, seems to have prevented the stone vault of the Antechapel from actually collapsing by having props erected. The roofs of the nave and transepts were of lead with wooden vaulting and there is a letter from Lloyd and Marychurch, the contractors who had worked on these roofs. They wrote to the Master of the Fabric in 1828 in no uncertain terms[26]:

> 'We do not hesitate to say that if it was at all wished to keep up the building, the roofs that you had us to repair could not with safety have been left undone………In many places the timbers are gone and that unless something effectually is done to them shortly some of the roofs will fall in.'

The Dean and Chapter were by no means idle in their care for the fabric during the first half of the nineteenth century. In 1846 an anonymous article appreared in Archaeologia Cambrensis which stated:

> 'We are glad to learn that the spirit of restoration has visited the metropolitical (sic) church of Wales……Great praise is due to the Dean and Chapter for the zeal and activity they have shown in the restoration of their venerable fabric, and their readiness to accept and second the efforts of those who have contributed to the repairs. Much remains to be done; we trust that this is but the beginning of a more complete restoration, and that it will hereafter be made the object of a diocesan or national subscription.'

These aspirations were to be realised just over fifteen years later when the Victorians grasped the nettle. Before that turning point, money was spent on lead for the roofs (£150) and a new organ (£700). In the North Transept the main window, which had long been blocked up, was renewed to a design by William Butterfield in 1846. The South Transept was fitted out as a parish church for the Welsh congregation. By this time, the position of Master of the Fabric was no longer an annual appointment and had become the responsibility of the Dean. From 1840 that post was held by Llewelyn Lewellin *(Fig. 15)*. He already had been appointed the first Principal of St Davids College, Lampeter in 1827, a position he was to hold, along with the Deanship, for 51 years until his death in 1878. Besides these two occupations, he was a magistrate, Vicar of Lampeter and also travelled widely. Inevitably, he was seldom at St Davids and rather neatly described as 'seventy miles absent'. As we shall see, he had a propensity for procrastination over Cathedral matters even when he was in residence.

In 1853, there was a public dispute in the form of four printed pamphlets about the distribution of Cathedral funds. The Master of the Cathedral School, Revd Nathaniel Davies, accused the Dean of not providing the school with the income which he was obliged to. His pamphlet[27] was innocently entitled 'Notes on the Cathedral Church of St David's' and it revealed the problem had been festering for at least eleven years. There was a reply by the Dean, followed by strictures on the Dean's reply by Davies and finally a reply again from the Dean. The details of this vitriolic and lengthy exchange need not concern us here, but the pamphlets do reveal the condition of the building and the expenditure on it at that time. In his first pamphlet, Davies says:

> 'The Tower is in a most dilapidated state, and several architects have pronounced it dangerous, calling for immediate attention. The roof of the North Transept for twelve years has had a leak which lets in gallons of water every shower of rain that falls, and five pounds would at first have made it watertight, if attention had been paid. The only remedy adopted was to bore a hole…….and now we have a water spout behind the organ whenever there is a heavy shower of rain.'

15 Dean Llewelyn Lewellin (Cathedral Library)

In his response Dean Lewellin lists the expenditure on the fabric during the thirteen years of his incumbency. He acknowledges the problems with the dilapidated state of the North Transept,

> 'but they have been of so serious an amount that, with the pressure of more necessary repairs in progress in other parts of the extensive building, we have as yet been obliged to postpone its reparation.'

He appears to be in denial about the condition of the Tower, does not 'participate in such alarm' and loftily says that 'with great confidence submit the whole of the case (i.e. his dispute with Nathaniel Davies) to the judgment of the Church and Public.'

The same haughty disregard of accountability on the part of Dean Lewellin was also revealed slightly earlier in 1851. In his other post as Principal of St Davids College in Lampeter he was criticised in a pamphlet[28] on two grounds. First, the academic standards and the student numbers had not been adequately maintained since the College had been opened in 1827. In particular the teaching of Welsh was deficient. Second, there was inadequate accounting of the income and expenditure of the College. When asked by the Treasury in Whitehall to provide these details for the period 1827 to 1850, Lewellin simply refused and only supplied data for 1847-1850. Twenty years of financial dealings were simply disregarded.

The Victorian Completion

Despite the efforts of the Dean and Chapter, by the middle of the nineteenth century the Cathedral was still in a ruinous and leaky state. To reiterate, there was a large crack in the Tower caused by the settlement of its western piers and there was the major loss of roofs over the Choir Aisles and eastern Chapels. The ingress of water generally was so serious that that George Gilbert Scott, the architect who was to be commissioned to undertake the final restoration, reported that:

> 'I do not hesitate to say that I have never witnessed anything approaching it in any other church. The walls, the pillars, and the floor, seem in damp weather perfectly saturated with wet, and after a few hours of heavy rain they, in many parts, literally stream with water.'

What were the factors which contributed to the crucial decision to begin a complete restoration of the Cathedral in the second half of the nineteenth century? One was a bequest of £2000 to the Cathedral in the will of Revd J. M. Traherne (nearly £200,000 in present value). He was a wealthy antiquarian and scholar from Cardiff, who died in 1860. There is a letter from Chancellor Melvill at St Davids showing that in 1851 Traherne had offered money for repair of the choir woodwork and the Bishop's throne[29]. To have done so when the roofs were so leaky would have been unwise to say the least (the words Titanic and deck chairs come to mind). Another factor was the publicity given by the publication in 1856 of The *History and Antiquities of St David's* by W. Basil Jones and Edward A. Freeman. This monumental work goes into great detail about the architectural fortunes of the Cathedral as well as its governance. The illustrations show the ruinous condition of the interior, as in *Figs 5* and *21* reproduced here. The book was published by subscription (over 200 are listed) and among those subscribing were Traherne, Scott, the Bishop of the Diocese and many influential persons of the time. In addition, the accessibility of St Davids from the rest of the kingdom was made easier by the extension of the rail network to Haverfordwest in 1854. But perhaps a much more generalised reason to act at this time was the greatly increased national prosperity based on the industrial revolution and world-wide trade, especially with the Empire. In other words, there was more money about.

The sixth of August, 1861 saw a turning point in the fortunes of St Davids Cathedral. On that day a special meeting of the Chapter was held. The draft record of the proceedings makes interesting reading. At first the Chapter Clerk wrote the following[30]:

> 'The Dean having produced to the Chapter a letter addressed to him, ordered and decreed that it be entered in the Minute Book......'.

There is a space in the draft and then there is a revised entry:

> 'Ordered and decreed that in accordance with the recommendation of the Bishop, a proper survey of the Cathedral be made without delay. Ordered and decreed that G. G. Scott Esq, 20 Spring Gardens London be employed for that purpose and that the Chapter Clerk be directed to communicate forthwith with Mr Scott'.

16 Bishop Connop Thirlwall (Cathedral Library)

It is tempting to surmise that the Dean was attempting to 'bury' the letter from the Bishop, but after discussion the Chapter decided to act upon it. In other words it was the Bishop who initiated what eventually became the final, complete restoration of the Cathedral, an echo of the same pressure by Bishop Horsley to restore the West Front seventy two years previously. The Bishop this time was Connop Thirlwall *(Fig.16),* appointed in the same year as Dean Lewellin, 1840. Thirlwall was a Cambridge scholar but no sheltered academic. Besides his diocesan responsibilities, he was heavily involved in affairs of church and state such as the Oxford Movement, the Disestablishment of the Irish Church

17 George Gilbert Scott (Cathedral Library)

and the Colenso Affair. He learnt Welsh and was able to preach to Welsh-speaking congregations. Over three decades he accomplished much in his large diocese besides restoring the cathedral, by encouraging the building of schools, repairing many churches and establishing a training college in Carmarthen. His burial in Westminster Abbey shows the high esteem in which he was held.

George Gilbert Scott *(Fig. 17)* was an extremely successful architect with probably the largest practice in the country. He had previously been to St Davids to sketch the cathedral for study and in lectures to the Royal Academy[31] he made it clear that he considered its beauties to be comparable to 'any from the neighbourhood of Paris, where the [Gothic] movement originated'. He was well known for his work on the design and restoration of churches. He had worked in every county in England and Wales, except Cardigan. In addition he had designed buildings in Canada, South Africa, New Zealand and Germany and in 1874 he was knighted for his design of the Albert Memorial in Hyde Park. Bishop Thirlwall had already engaged him in 1860 for the restoration of Brecon Priory Church (now Cathedral).

Scott's 1862 Report to the Dean and Chapter[32] on the state of the Fabric, running to 32 printed pages, spelt out how crucial it was to deal first and foremost with the tower:

> 'The present condition of the Tower is in the highest degree alarming, and until it is restored to a state of security, it is quite useless to think of any reparation of other parts of the building.'

There is a striking drawing in Pugin's series which shows the state of the Tower at that time *(Fig.11)*. It shows the ominous crack in the south face as well as similar problems with the South Transept. The crack must have been the result of weakness in the western piers of the Tower *(Fig. 1)* following the rebuilding after the collapse in the thirteenth century, as we have already seen. The two western piers of the tower would have to be rebuilt while temporarily supporting the weight they were carrying by means of massive wooden shoring. His first experience of this type of work was at St Mary's, Stafford some twenty years earlier and he had successfully repaired several other towers. Nevertheless Scott felt that St Davids tower was the largest, most difficult and hazardous one he had undertaken. When asked how confident he was of a successful outcome, he wrote, somewhat guardedly, to the Chapter Clerk that:

> '.....though I hold myself bound to give all my skill to the successful execution of that work and am confident of success, I wish it to be understood that I do not hold myself in any degree pecuniarily responsible but, like a physician, do my best and assure you of my confidence of success but do not go further than this.'[31]

He pointed out that the tower had been partly prevented from falling by the support it had from the adjoining walls of the nave and the two transepts. This pressure had caused westward movement of the nave with damage to the adjoining stonework which would also have to be repaired. The nave itself needed repairs to its clerestory, roof and aisles; both transepts needed new roofs with oak vaulting and a great deal of internal work; the presbytery required extensive repairs to its roof timbers and renewal of its east window. The window was of Perpendicular design and is shown in *Fig.6,* which also shows the sad condition of the roofless eastern parts of the building, sprouting a vigorous growth of weeds.

Other areas in need of attention were the South Porch, St Thomas' Chapel with the building over it (now the Library) and the general provision of lighting and heating. Scott estimated that all this could be accomplished for the sum of £25,000 – 30,000. When the accounts were made up in 1877 he was shown to have been remarkably accurate: the expenditure to that time was £30,412.

Once Scott's Report had been circulated to the members of the Chapter, a Special Meeting was called in April 1862 to consider how to proceed. Members of the Chapter seem to have split into two factions: those who wanted to restrict work to the tower alone and those who were in favour of the restoration of the whole building. We know this because a fascinating series of letters which the clergy wrote to the Chapter Clerk, a local solicitor, have survived. As always, money was the key factor. Canon W.B. Thomas, the Canon Treasurer, wrote[33]

18 Chancellor Sir Erasmus Williams (Cathedral Library)

complaining that the Chapter was:

'so divided a House at St Davids.....and that we shall be succeeded by a generation more united and more energetic than the present one is.' Canon Harries wrote[34] rather despairingly that: 'I have only to wish we had the means of accomplishing all he suggests. In my opinion it is quite a hopeless affair.' A prominent member of the Chapter was the Chancellor, Revd Sir Erasmus Williams, Bart *(Fig 18)*. He was a cantankerous and outspoken critic of the Dean and a robust champion for complete restoration. He criticised the Dean's cautious approach saying[35]:

'The Public Voice is anxiously waiting our decision whether we are in earnest or not, & it is very certain that the Public will button up their breeches pockets if a mere bolstering up of the tower is only intended. Preparation must be made for the whole restoration & we had better retire with our tails between our legs at once than become the laughing stock of the world.'

The Chapter Clerk was instructed to write to the two Government bodies which might have funds, the Exchequer Loan Commissioners and the Ecclesiastical Commissioners. Neither was immediately forthcoming but the Ecclesiastical Commissioners at least agreed[36] to 'lay it [the Report] on the table' and, several years later, did provide a substantial grant.

Even though the decision had been taken to proceed, there were still doubts about whether it would actually happen. Erasmus Williams writes to the Chapter Clerk in May, 1862[37]:

'I wish the Dean would cut away to any place but this, for with him I fear little will be done & without him there would be no difficulty...... This cursed love of money is the bane of all righteousness & the Dean has it in perfection. Between ourselves, R [Canon Richardson] thinks nothing will be done unless the Bishop visits the Chapter. It really is quite horrible when the Dean's reluctance to move at all, after the many thousands he has drawn from this Cathedral...... There is an epitaph on a person in these words

Whether he lives or whether he dies
Nobody laughs and nobody cries
Where he is gone and how he fares
Nobody knows and nobody cares

It is not inappropriate to another who shall be nameless........ We are a shabby lot'

Eventually, having Traherne's bequest and the promise of personal contributions from the Bishop and members of the Chapter, a fund-raising meeting was called in Carmarthen in October, 1863 which was attended by the great and the good from the area. Although the Dean was present he does not appear to have spoken. The principal speakers were the Bishop and Scott himself. Their speeches were later printed for fund-raising purposes. The Bishop made an impassioned plea, regretting how difficult it was to raise interest in the Cathedral because of its isolated position:

'I have myself often been asked by persons of education whether there is such a building as the Cathedral of St David's......It is true the old city and Cathedral receive occasional visitors, but they are comparatively rare. It is an excursion which is often looked upon as a kind of adventure, like the discovery of an Alpine pass.'

He threw his weight behind a total restoration rather than just the Tower by saying:

'Shall we be really carrying out the intentions of this noble bequest [Traherne's] if this £2000 is to be buried in the foundation of the Tower. I think the bequest ought rather to be returned to the representatives of the testator before a single shilling was spent in so ignoble, so disgraceful, a misuse.'

Scott, in his speech, emphasized:

'....the dreadful state it is in.....Its unseemliness, its dampness, its forlorn condition, are beyond description. When I was there taking my survey, the wall and pavements were literally streaming with water.'

Following this meeting, the subscription list was published in the Pembrokeshire Herald of March 4, 1864 and repeated in 29 issues during the year. Presumably this was a tactic for shaming the public into subscribing and demonstrating the largesse of those who had. By the end of the year, the list contained 236 names and the total raised was just over £9000. With this support, the authorities felt confident enough to put the work out to tender. The reply of Joseph Wood & Son of Worcester was accepted in October, 1864. The Agreement between the Dean and Chapter and the contractor was split into four parts[38]. Division 1 (for £10,094), comprising work on the lower parts of the tower and the presbytery (roof and east window) was to be started together with Division 4 (for £544) which provided proper drainage for the whole site. The rest of the Agreement for work on the upper part of the tower (Division 2, £2,355) and for the restitution of the choir aisles and arcades (Division 3, £3,363), was to be carried out at a later date.

In his *Recollections*[39], Scott admits that restoring ruined towers was not the most pleasurable aspect of his practise, for he describes it as: '…. dangerous work, which it has since been my too frequent lot to repeat, and a most unenviable lot it is'.

He lays down several principles for the benefit of those who have to undertake similar work.

I. Be assured that no amount of shoring can be too much for safety and no foundations to your shoring too strong, and no principles of constructing it too well considered.

II. Use the hardest stone for your new work which you can procure, and spare no pains in bonding it and tying it together with copper.

III. Be very slow in your operations……..be careful in your principle of moveable supports, as you cut away old work; set every stone in the very best cement and run in the core with grout of the same material.

IV. Key up well at the top and leave your shoring a long time after the work is done, and then remove it with the greatest care.

V. Tie your tower well together with iron before you begin…..Above all, have a thoroughly practical clerk of the works, neither too young, nor too old.

How he carried these principles into practice can be seen in his original drawings for St Davids. One of them is reproduced here *(Fig 19)*. It shows the very extensive area of concrete foundations which had to be laid and also some of the massive timbers needed to prop up the tower while two of its four piers were being replaced. In essence, the task was to temporarily

19 Part of Scott's drawing showing his method for supporting the north-western pier of the tower during its reconstruction. Note the extensive and deep footings which had to be dug well below the existing floor level (thick stepped line). The manikin represents a 6 ft human to scale (Supplied by Llyfrgel Genedlaethol Cymru/National Library of Wales)

support the immense weight of the tower so that the two western piers could be replaced with new stone. First, the northern and western arches were supported with strong wooden framing. Next, huge inclined shores were put up both internally and externally to prevent any lateral movement. The upper part of the tower was bound together with internal and external wooden framing and twelve permanent iron tie-rods still to be seen *(Fig.2)*. With all this support in place, holes were carefully cut through the north-western pier to enable horizontal 'needles' of oak to be inserted. These needles were bundles of timber bound together with iron straps to form immensely strong wooden girders measuring 2ft 4in square in section. The ends of the needles were supported by vertical props. In this way the weakened pier could be supported so that the stone below the needle could be safely removed and replaced. The process was repeated at a higher level and in this way the whole pier was gradually renewed. Having secured the support for the north-western corner of the tower, the workmen moved across to the south-western pier. Here the state of the masonry was in an equally dangerous state so that 'a cat could walk in and out the cracks'. Again, proceeding with great caution, this pier was replaced by May 1866. The whole process had been fraught with difficulties and danger. Operations were supervised by Scott's Clerk of the Works, Mr J. B. Clear. Scott pays fulsome tribute to Clear's devotion:

> 'I can truly say that no expression I can make use of can overstate the amount of attention, study, and judgment, he has brought to bear upon the work, and that in the absence of any great amount of that encouragement and sympathy, which in a less secluded place would have cheered him on under the load of arduous and wearing anxiety he had so long to endure.'

Clear stood beneath the tower when the final supports were removed saying that 'if the tower fell he would be smashed first'[40]. Back in his London office, Scott admitted that he could hardly open a letter from St Davids without trepidation that it might bring bad news.

For the tower restoration huge quantities of timber were used. The total volume was 12,000 cubic feet or, in terms more easy to comprehend, equivalent to the volume of 150 old GPO telephone boxes (incidentally, designed by Scott's grandson Giles Gilbert Scott). The organ, the furnishings in the choir and the ends of the organ screen had to be removed so the disruption must have been considerable. Small wonder that Erasmus Williams wrote of the need for a 'chapel of ease' where worship could continue during the work[41].

There was one unexpected outcome: in making the excavations for the foundations of the shoring, it was necessary to disturb 'several graves of ancient bishops'. These were probably those of Bishops Carew (1256-1280) and Bec (1280-1293) Apart from the bones, which were carefully reinterred, a group of artefacts was retrieved and can now be seen in the new Treasury (part of the Millennium Restoration). They include two silver chalices, three coins and three gold amethyst rings.

The stone required was extracted from the original quarry in the cliffs at Caerbwdy which is only a mile or so from the Cathedral *(Fig 14)*. Recently the same quarry was reopened to provide stone for the Millennium Project when the Cloister was rebuilt and the scene must have been very like that shown in *Fig 20*. The large baulks of timber (36 ft long) were another matter. Although the railway had reached Haverfordwest by then, there was still the difficult journey of 16 miles to St Davids by road. As in Nash's time, the much closer inlet at Porth Clais could well have been used but no port records have survived. The source of lead for the roofs was apparently not the local mines in Pembrokeshire or in Cardiganshire but from

20 Photograph showing the removal of stone from the cliff-face quarry at Caerbwdy for the rebuilding of the Cloister in 1997 (courtesy Philip Clarke)

21 Two views of the Presbytery. Above, before Scott's restoration (Jones & Freeman p 67) showing ugly extra supports for the roof. Right, as it appears today (author photo)

Cornwall and/or Derbyshire. The local historian, Roy Lewis, found lead pellets in fields around the Cathedral which most likely came from the ashes of fires used to cast or re-cast the lead sheets before they were laid on the roofing timbers. He had samples analysed for lead isotope ratios and the results left no doubt that they came from Cornwall and Derbyshire. Again it is likely that the Cornish lead would have come in through Porth Clais.

In 1866, with the tower secured, it was necessary to raise more funds. Canon W. B. Thomas who wrote to the Chapter Clerk from his vicarage in rather despairing terms[42]:

> 'I am sorry to say that Mr Chalk [from the Ecclesiastical Commissioners] is able to give us no assistance in the matter of raising money for the restoration of the Cathedral. Would the Board of Works advance us money on the security of our Canonical Income & the tithes of Uzmaston? If not, possibly the Governors of Queen Anne's Bounty would. But somehow or another we must 'ere long get money for the purpose by either borrowing or begging.'

This was in March 1866. By June he must have gone up to London to see the Commissioners in person, for he writes from a Euston Square address to say that he has had two long conversations with Chalk[43]. The result was good news: the Commissioners were now prepared to offer a grant of £10,000 on suitable security.

Work continued on restoring the roof of the Presbytery which at that time was propped up with rather ugly supports *(Fig 21)* because the main beams were rotten. To find oak of such massive size proved difficult. Eventually they were sourced from Radnorshire, Shropshire, Herefordshire and the Forest of Dean. The finished ceiling was painted like the original, and displayed the arms of the Bishop, Dean, Canons and Archdeacons at that time.

As *Fig 21* shows, the single eastern window of the Presbytery was in the Perpendicular style and its stonework was badly decayed. Scott planned to replace it with four lancets corresponding to those which had originally been here. Below these windows and immediately behind the high altar, were three much larger openings now blocked by Holy Trinity Chapel. In his First Report, Scott had advised some form of durable decoration for these and eventually the solution was to fill the spaces with glass mosaics. The woodwork in the Choir, all of which had to be removed to allow work on the tower to be done, was carefully restored. As already mentioned, money for this had been offered as early as 1851 by Traherne. The Canon's stalls had a fine collection of twenty eight misericords[44]. These were put in good order and in a few cases replaced. Two of the replacements carry the arms of Dean Lewellin and Bishop Thirlwall. Likewise the imposing Bishop's Throne and the wooden parclose screen between the Choir and Presbytery were restored.

Having secured the piers of the tower, the builders proceeded to repair its two external upper tiers and the parapet. The process can be seen in *Fig 22*, which is one of very few photographs illustrating the restoration. The internal wooden roof (vault) of the tower gave Scott some difficulty. The existing vault was at a height which cut across half of the main tower windows. After some deliberation, he decided to install a new vault at a level above these windows to admit more light; the resulting painted ceiling can still be admired today *(Fig 23)*.

More light could also be admitted to the Presbytery when the roofs of the north and south choir aisles were once again put in place, enabling the blocked arches shown in *Figs 5 & 21* to be opened.

22 View from the west during Scott's restoration of building work on the North Transept and the parapet of the Tower (courtesy Peter B S Davies)

23 Tower vault inserted by Scott (author photo)

24 Bishop Basil Jones (Cathedral Library)

The entrance to the Choir from the Nave through the rood screen was by 'a rough and uncouth archway'. On investigating the roof and sides of this archway Scott uncovered some beautiful medieval paintings and revealed a particularly fine stone vault over this passageway. This small discovery gave him special pleasure for he says:

'this beautiful addition to the entrance to the Choir was wholly beyond anything I had anticipated'.

At this stage in the restoration work, Scott wrote his Second Report to the Bishop, Dean and Chapter[45] which describes in some detail what had been accomplished in the seven years to 1869 and went on to list all the reparations still needed. We have already seen what had been achieved by this time and now need to consider the formidable amount of work which still remained before the Cathedral could be regarded as fully restored. Scott recommended that the interior work should be done as completely as possible, while only essential repairs should be made to the exterior so that services would be disturbed as little as possible. The nave together with its aisles needed major work, particularly on the main roof, 'or the congregation would often have to walk up the Church under umbrellas'. The floor of the nave would have to be replaced too and in addition the South Porch needed restoring. Further eastwards the two transepts needed new roofs. A contemporary photograph *(Fig 22)* shows that at that time the ridges of their roofs were much lower than after restoration, coming well below the height of the gable. Next, the part comprising St Thomas Chapel and the Library above needed much work to its roof, windows and interior.

Finally, to this daunting list he added the desirability of installing heating and lighting systems. Scott is optimistic that:

'the inhabitants of this rich and important Diocese…. will gladly come forward to complete the restoration of the most historical, the most nationally typical, the most beautiful and in every way the most valuable ecclesiastical building in the Principality.'

He concludes his Second Report with an astonishing outburst, which looks totally out of order. Although an Englishman, he evidently felt strongly that the Welsh congregation was being neglected in the Cathedral:

'I protest against the more national part of the congregation being thrust aside into a transept. I claim for them, if not the Choir, at least the Nave. Let the Dean and Chapter, with the English-speaking inhabitants, occupy the Choir; but let the Nave….be held by the more national inhabitants, and let them have their own People's Altar, and all that is necessary to render the services of their Cathedral and Diocesan Church as perfect, as dignified, and as noble in every way as those of the Choir. Without this your restoration will be one but in vain.'

There does not seem to be any record of how the clergy responded to this attempt to tell them how to run their cathedral, though it is not hard to imagine the reaction.

Bishop Thirlwall retired in 1874 and died one year later. He was followed as Bishop by Basil Jones *(Fig 24)* who had so many connections with St Davids as well as writing the Cathedral's history as a young man. In 1878, Dean Lewellin died and was succeeded by James Allen *(Fig 25)*. He had first come to St Davids in 1870 as Canon Residentiary, then became Chancellor and, at the age of 76, he was appointed Dean. He became the first resident Dean, holding the position until he

25 Dean James Allen being taken for a drive around the Close (Cathedral Library)

was 93. Allen had previously spent thirty five years as Vicar of Castlemartin, Pembrokeshire where he had personally supervised the restoration of that church, using local builders. He was a thoroughly practical man and is said to have built a wall at his father's rectory in his youth. Despite his age, there could not have been a greater contrast with his predecessor. He not only vigorously pursued the restoration process but also contributed considerable amounts of his own funds.

These changes meant that from the latter half of the 1870's there was a new impetus in Cathedral affairs. In 1877 the accounts of the Restoration Fund were published. They reveal that many of the recommendations in Scott's Second Report had been carried through. There were two important private contributions to the fund. First the Rev. John Lucy paid for the stained glass in Scott's new east windows in the Presbytery and the mosaics above the High Altar. Dean Allen himself made the large contribution of £2992 which was used, among other things, for the new roof of the North Transept and the Chapter House above St Thomas Chapel. According to one of his obituaries, 'he chose and examined the materials used, and would undertake long journeys to inspect the timber and other requisites for the repairs; even the very mortar was subject to his scrutiny; and words cannot describe the thought and care he bestowed on the minutest details and the extraordinary technical knowledge which he brought to bear upon the work.' The same source shows that he also arranged the paving of the nave with Italian marble, which was imported through Porth Clais. Not content with this devotion to the Fabric, he arranged for the old books in the Cathedral Library to be rebound, by bringing a bookbinder to work in St Davids. All in all, a remarkable contribution for a man of his age. At his death in 1897 he had survived to see the whole restoration completed, except for the Eastern Chapels.

As a memorial to Bishop Thirlwall, who had done so much to initiate and oversee the process of restoration, it was proposed that Scott should produce a new design for the West Front to replace Nash's one of the 1790s. There was to be a niche above the West Door holding a statue of Thirlwall. Scott's drawing is reproduced in *Fig 26* along with a modern day photograph. It seems that the design was not adhered to completely. The drawing shows a new gable end with a steep pitch angle (51 degrees) which matches the medieval pitch of the nave roof, still to be seen on the west face of the tower. This would have involved rebuilding the nave roof to match the gable. Clearly this was not done and the gable was reduced to match the existing roof pitch. The architect died in 1878 and he never lived to see his design executed. However he did pay a visit to St Davids shortly before his death because there are photographs showing Scott, Bishop Jones (appointed 1874), Dean Allen and Professor Freeman at the Cathedral. One is reproduced here *(Fig 27)*. It is likely that the occasion was a site-visit to decide the fate of the West Front.

The necessary funds must have been raised locally but initially they were insufficient. Bishop Jones, in a sermon in 1877[46], reveals that there was only enough to replace the central part of the West Front leaving the undesirable compromise

26 Scott's drawing for the West Front is shown above (© Crown Copyright: Royal Commission on Ancient and Historic Monuments Wales) and below how it appears today (author photo)

27 Group taken in the North Choir Aisle about 1876. The lighting shows that there was no roof. The men from left to right are Sir Gilbert Scott, Professor E A Freeman, Bishop Jones and Dean Allen. The man on the extreme right holding dividers bears a strong similarity to the corresponding figure in Fig 28, taken about 25 years later (Cathedral Library)

of a design mixing Nash and Scott on the same part of the cathedral. Meanwhile, in Cambridge there had been a proposal for another memorial to Thirlwall: a new Chair in History was to be founded. The funds for endowing that Chair were evidently also not sufficient, because in 1882, a meeting was held in the Master's Lodge of Trinity College, Cambridge where it was proposed to transfer those funds to the St Davids appeal. The printed pamphlet describing the proceedings of the meeting[47] also reveals that the Rev. Traherne's widow left a bequest to the Cathedral which matched that of her husband viz. £2000. Her name is on a ceiling bracket in the north aisle of the nave along with the coat of arms of her family (the Talbots of Margam).

Approaching the end of the 19th century, the only remaining parts of the Cathedral yet to be restored were the Lady Chapel and the aisles leading to it past Holy Trinity Chapel. The Chapter, now led by Dean Howell after the deaths of Deans Allen and Phillips, called on Gilbert Scott's son, John Oldrid Scott, to make a report on the work which remained. His 11 page hand-written report of 1897 is preserved in the National Library[48].

He concludes:

> 'It is a work deserving the earnest efforts of the Chapter, as well as of the whole Diocese. The Cathedral has hitherto been dealt with, with a loving and generous hand, and this concluding work should not fall short of what has already been so successfully accomplished.'

28 Group of workmen building the eastern end of the Lady Chapel taken about 1899 (Cathedral Library)

The estimated cost was £5600. Once again, and this time finally, an appeal was launched by Dean Howell in 1898.

There is a splendid photograph of the workmen on the Lady Chapel which is reproduced in *Fig 28*. The Chapel received a new stone vault and the roofs of the remaining parts of the North and South Choir Aisles were completed. Oldrid Scott's design included a statue of the Madonna and Child above the east window and the two beautiful heads at the base of its architrave depicted in *Fig 29*.

A service to commemorate the opening of the Lady Chapel was held in October 1901. The sermon was preached by the Bishop of Exeter on the text: 'The House that fell not'. The printed version of the sermon[49] shows that he appeared to be unaware of the fact that they were actually celebrating the end of one hundred and ten years of almost unremitting fund-raising and building. It all began with that crucial letter from Bishop Horsley to the Chapter in 1789 which initiated the saving of St Davids Cathedral to give us the magnificent building we see today.

Another century was to pass before there was any further significant work on the cathedral fabric. At the turn of the 20th century, on the initiative of Dean (now Bishop) Wyn Evans, the cloister was built, the organ was rebuilt and the Refectory was created in St Mary's Hall. But that is another story.

29 Madonna and Child above the east window of the Lady Chapel and two faces on the window tracery (author photo)

Bibliography

MANY OF THE REFERENCES ARE FROM TWO SOURCES AND THESE WILL ABBREVIATED:

J & F indicates Jones, W. B. & Freeman E. A. *The History and Antiquities of St David's* London: Parker, Smith and Petheram 1856

NLW indicates National Library of Wales, Aberystwyth. Here the majority of sources are to be found under the heading: *CHURCH IN WALES: DIOCESE OF ST DAVIDS EPISCOPAL 4* and within this collection SDCh/B indicates chapter act books, SDCh/LET indicates letters and SDCh/Misc indicates miscellaneous documents.

1   J & F, p 146

2   J & F, p 151

3   Evans, W. *The Reformation and St Davids Cathedral* J. Welsh Eccl. Hist. Vol 7 pp 1-16, (1990)

4   John, T. *The Civil War in Pembrokeshire* Woonton Almeley, Herefordshire: Logaston Press (2008)

5   Charles, B. G. *A Calendar of the Records of the Borough of Haverfordwest 1539-1660* Cardiff: Univ. Wales Press 1967

6   Yardley, E. *Menevia Sacra* ed. Francis Green p.13. London: Bedford Press for the Cambian Archeological Association (1927)

7   Evans, W. *St Davids Cathedral: the forgotten centuries* J. Welsh Eccl. Hist. Vol 3 pp 73-92 (1986)

8   J & F, p 83 footnote 'o'.

9   NLW SDCh/Misc/210

10   J & F, p 173

11   J & F, p 174

12   Evans, J. Wyn Personal communication

13   Pugin, A. W. N. *Contrasts; or, a parallel between the noble edifices of the fourteenth and fifteenth centuries and similar buildings of the present day* Salisbury: publ. by the author (1836)

14   NLW SDCh/LET/7

15   NLW SDCh/B/8

16   Jones, I. Wyn *Architectural Rev.* Vol 112 pp 63-65 (1952)

17   NLW SDCh/Misc/214

18   J & F p 177

19   NLW SDCh/Misc/217

20   NLW SDCh/Misc/226

21   NLW SDCh/LET/117

22   J & F p 176

23   NLW SDCh/LET/107

24   Thomas, J. E. *Britain's last invasion, Fishguard 1797* Stroud: Tempus (2007)

25   NLW SDCh/Misc/217

26   NLW SDCh/LET/220

27   Davies, N. *Notes on the Cathedral Church of St David's* London: Simpkin, Marshall (1853)

28   Anon *St David's College Lampeter: its assailants and its defenders* London: Partridge and Oakey (1851)

29   NLW 6599E/LET/256

30   NLW SDCh/Misc/236

31   Scott, G. G. *Lectures on the rise and fall of medieval architecture* London: John Murray (1879)

32   Scott, G. G. *Report made by order of the Dean and Chapter on the state of the Fabric of St David's Cathedral* Tenby: R. Mason (1862)

33   NLW SDCh/LET/420

34   NLW SDCh/LET/422

35   NLW SDCh/LET/427

36   NLW SDCh/LET/428

37   NLW SDCh/LET/431

38   NLW SDCh/Misc/239

39   Scott, G. G. *Personal and professional recollections* A Facsimile of the Original Edition with New Material and a Critical Introduction by Gavin Stamp. Stamford: Paul Watkins (1995)

40   Anon *The Builder* June 23, 1866, p 471

41   NLW SDCh/LET/475 and 480

42   NLW SDCh/LET/515

43   NLW SDch/LET/516

44   Rees, N. *The Misericords of St Davids Cathedral* Much Wenlock: R. J. L. Smith and Associates (2007)

45   Scott G. G. *A second report on the state of the fabric of St David's Cathedral made by order of the Committee for the Restoration* London: J. Parker (1869)

46   *Pembrokeshire Herald* November 2, 1877

47   Pembrokeshire Record Office HDX/894/3

48   NLW SDCh/Misc/243

49   Pembrokeshire Record Office HDX/894/5